KNOW IT ALL

PIRATES

Philip Steele

W

FRANKLIN WATTS

LONDON • SYDNEY

First published in 2013
by Franklin Watts

Copyright © Franklin Watts 2013

Franklin Watts
338 Euston Road
London NW1 3BH

Franklin Watts Australia
Level 17/207 Kent Street
Sydney, NSW 2000

Series Editor: Amy Stephenson
Planning and production by Discovery Books Ltd
Editor: James Nixon
Series Designer: D.R. ink
Picture researcher: James Nixon
Picture credits: cover image (artincamera/Shutterstock).
Alamy: pp. 16 (Lebrecht Music and Arts Photo Library), 21 (Mary Evans Picture Library), 25 (Andrew Holt). Bigstock: p. 11 top (dzain). Bridgeman Art Library: pp. 4 bottom (Look and Learn), 15 top and bottom (Peter Newark Historical Pictures), 18 (Peter Newark Historical Pictures), 19 bottom (Peter Newark Historical Pictures). Getty Images: pp. 9 bottom (Candela Foto Art/Kreuziger), 14 top (Candela Foto Art/ Kreuziger), 26 bottom (Veronique de Viguerie/Edit). Istockphoto: p. 22 top (Manuel Velasco). Photoshot: pp. 29 top (Starstock), 29 bottom (Walt Disney Pictures). Shutterstock: pp. 2 and 7 bottom (Horimono), 4 top (Joseph Scott Photography), 5 (meunierd), 6 (ilolab), 9 top (Jeanne McRight), 10 bottom-left (Anna Subbotina), 10 bottom-right (Lori Labrecque), 11 bottom (Fer Gregory), 13 bottom (Pres Panayotov), 19 top (great_photos), 22 bottom (Fer Gregory), 23 top (Jonathan Cooke), 24 bottom (Thorsten Schmitt). Wikimedia: pp. 7 top (Google Art Project), 8, 10 top (Miriam Thyes), 11 middle, 12 top, 12 bottom (Rama), 13 top (Rama), 14 bottom, 17 top and bottom, 20 top, middle and bottom, 23 bottom, 24 top, 26 top (Michal Manas), 27 top (Eric L Beauregard/US Navy), 27 bottom (Herbert D Banks Jr/US Navy), 28.

Dewey number 910.4'5
ISBN ISBN 978 1 4451 1823 9

Printed in China

Franklin Watts is a division of Hachette Children's Books, an Hachette UK company.
www.hachette.co.uk

CONTENTS

All words in **bold** can be found in the glossary on page 31.

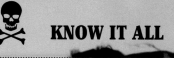

PIRATES AHOY!

A cry from the lookout brings the captain running from his cabin. An unknown ship can be seen on the stormy horizon. As it sails nearer, it runs a black-and-white flag up the mast. This shows the blood-chilling sign of the **skull-and-crossbones**... Prepare for an attack by PIRATES!

SEA RAIDERS

Pirates are violent sea raiders. They attack or capture other ships, stealing gold, jewellery, weapons or other **cargo**. They may take prisoners and demand **ransoms**. Sometimes they **plunder** towns and harbours along the coast.

The most famous pirate attacks took place in the 1600s and 1700s, but pirates have actually been causing death and destruction at sea for thousands of years – and they still are today.

AMAZING FACT
It's an old, old story

The word 'pirate' goes back to ancient Greece over 2,500 years ago. Back then *peirates* meant a 'chancer' or 'attacker'. Other names for pirates over the ages have included corsair, buccaneer, rover, filibuster, freebooter and sea beggar.

Pirates rush to move their stolen treasure on to the shore.

DESPERATE AND DANGEROUS

What sort of people became pirates? Many were mean and dangerous people. They included brutal murderers, cruel torturers and greedy thieves. Some pirates were very poor people in search of a fortune. Some were daring adventurers, rebels, escaped prisoners or slaves. Others were sailors who had run away from the harsh **discipline** of the navy.

On their own ships, pirates chose a captain for themselves and were able to make their own rules. And they were free to terrorise the world.

TRUE OR FALSE?

Women were banned from all pirate ships. **True or False?**

FALSE! Sailors often believed that a woman on board ship brought bad luck. Some pirates followed this rule, but on a few ships women were among the fiercest fighters of all. Mary Read and Anne Bonny fought alongside 'Calico' Jack Rackham around about 1720. Anne was an Irish woman who ran off with Jack. Mary was English. She had fought as a soldier, dressed as a man. When her ship was captured by Rackham's pirates, she joined up with them.

Pirates were ruthless, dangerous people who were happy to kill the victims that they attacked and robbed.

THE SEVEN SEAS

In ancient times seafarers used to talk about 'sailing the Seven Seas'. Today we know there are over a hundred seas, and that at one time or another in history, pirates have sailed most of them.

The ancient Greeks and Romans knew all about piracy. In 78BCE the Roman Emperor Julius Caesar was captured by pirates in the Mediterranean. As soon as his ransom was paid, he made sure they were all rounded up and killed.

TRUE OR FALSE?

Pirates invented the barbecue. **True or False?**

TRUE! – WELL SORT OF! The first buccaneers took their name from the word *buccan*, a wooden frame used for smoking meat over a slow fire. These pirates hunted cattle and pigs on the Caribbean island of Hispaniola, which today is shared by two countries – Haiti and the Dominican Republic. The modern word barbecue also has Caribbean roots – *barabicu* meant a 'fire pit'.

North-west Europe 800s-1500s

Eastern Mediterranean 1400BCE-67BCE

Atlantic Coast 1700s

Bermuda

Barbary Coast 1500s-1800s

South China Sea 1800s-1930s

Caribbean 1500s-1700s

Persian Gulf 1700s-1800s

Spanish Main 1600s

Somali Coast 2000s

Pirate Round

Madagascar 1600s-1700s

AMAZING FACT
Terror from the sea

The first pirate attacks on record were carried out by fierce raiders known as the 'Sea People', over 3,400 years ago in the eastern Mediterranean.

Pirates have probably sailed the world's oceans and seas ever since boats were invented. Here are the locations of some famous periods of pirate activity.

BARBARY CORSAIRS

From the 1500s, the Barbary Coast of North Africa, around Algeria, was swarming with pirates called corsairs. Most were Muslim Arabs, the local Berber people or Turks, but they were also later joined by Dutch and English pirates. The newcomers were welcomed by the corsairs because of their experience of the stormier Atlantic waters. The corsairs' **galleys** attacked rich merchant vessels and even the Pope's treasure ships.

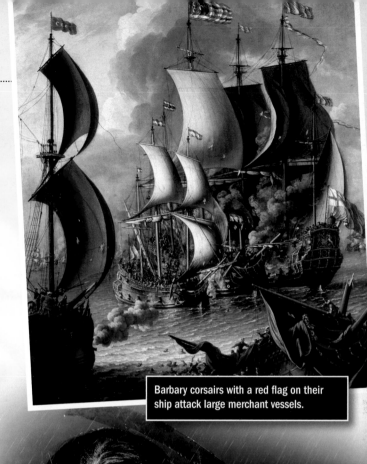

Barbary corsairs with a red flag on their ship attack large merchant vessels.

THE SPANISH MAIN

After the Spanish invaded the Americas in the 1500s and 1600s, they shipped stolen gold, silver and emeralds back to Europe in big ships called galleons. Their fleets were preyed upon in turn by pirates called buccaneers. These outlaws hid away on small Caribbean Islands. Buccaneer armies also raided the Spanish-ruled mainland in Central and South America, known as the Spanish Main.

SAILING EAST

By the 1690s, pirates were sailing from Bermuda in the North Atlantic Ocean to West Africa, Madagascar and the Indian Ocean, returning with their spoils to ports in North America. This route was known as the 'Pirate Round'. In the 1800s, large pirate fleets were based around the Persian Gulf in the Middle East and in the South China Sea.

Pirates often attacked ships at night. They climbed aboard and killed sailors before the alarm could be raised.

A DEADLY BUSINESS

A pirate sells his jewels to a rich merchant.

Being a pirate was a dangerous business, with the very real possibility of being killed in action, or being caught and hanged. But for men and women who didn't fit – or didn't want to fit – into ordinary life at home, 'going on the account' (becoming a pirate) and raiding shipping offered the possibility of huge wealth and a wild, luxury lifestyle. Pirates could make big profits by selling their plunder in secret to rich merchants.

THE PRIVATEERS

Seafarers called privateers were given official permission to attack and plunder the ships of enemy nations. Their licences to do this were called **letters of marque**. Privateers could claim that they were not real pirates, but to their victims, lying in a pool of blood, it made precious little difference.

AMAZING FACT
Hero or villain?

Piracy has always been a **lucrative** business. The English 'seadog' Francis Drake sailed around the world in the 1570s, attacking many Spanish ships. The gold he took from just one of them would be worth about £7 million today. When he returned home, Drake was welcomed by Queen Elizabeth I and knighted – but the Spanish always despised him as a common pirate.

THE PIRATE CODE

Pirates had certain rules. Even rowdy pirate crews drew up agreements amongst themselves, and forced their captives to sign up as well. Pirates would swear to be loyal, to share out treasure fairly, to look after their weapons and not to fight each other. Needless to say, these rules were often forgotten in drunken brawls. In 1718 one of the craziest captains of all, Edward Teach or Blackbeard, casually shot his second-in-command in the kneecap – just a gentle reminder of who was boss.

Pirates often agreed a kind of insurance policy. If you were injured in battle, you would receive a payment – so much for an eye, so much for an arm, so much if you needed a peg for your leg. Buccaneers in the 1600s could be given up to 600 pieces-of-eight (silver coins) for the loss of a limb, but only 100 pieces-of-eight for the loss of an eye.

Pirates wore an eyepatch if they lost or injured an eye.

TRUE OR FALSE?

Pirates were always attacking other pirate crews. **True or False?**

FALSE! Generally, one pirate ship would not attack another. Each would prepare for action if an unknown vessel approached. If the ship ran up a pirate flag, the other crew would just fire off their cannon as a salute, and sail on by.

Sharing out the treasure between shipmates would often end in fights and arguments.

SHIPS FROM HELL

The first thing a pirate needed was a ship. Sometimes ordinary sailors **mutinied** against their captain. Then they took over the ship and became pirates. Often pirates captured other ships at sea. In this way they could form a pirate fleet.

The most useful pirate ships were always the ones which were small enough to hide away in **creeks** and coves, and nippy enough to make a quick getaway.

PIRATE JOKE

Q Why is it hard to play cards on a pirate ship?

A Because the captain keeps standing on the deck!

GALLEYS AND SLOOPS

Pirates used all sorts of ships over the ages. The Barbary corsairs had fast galleys, rowed by their captives, who were lashed with whips. The pirates of the Arabian Sea sailed wooden **dhows**, fine ships with triangular sails. Chinese pirate gangs had **junks**, sturdy ships with their sails stiffened by **battens**.

Galley

The first buccaneers of the Caribbean used small sailing canoes to attack the slow and bulky Spanish galleons. Pirate **sloops** of the 1700s had single masts and sails to send them skimming over the waves. Two-masted **schooners** and **brigantines** of the 1800s carried lots of sail to catch the wind and help them chase down their victims.

Junk

Sloop

Brigantine

BENEATH THE WAVES

Many pirate ships were wrecked in storms. The *Whydah* sank one dark night off Cape Cod, Massachusetts, USA, in 1717. This ship, carrying 60 or more cannon and over four tonnes of gold and silver, had been captured by pirate chief 'Black Sam' Bellamy. Over 100 drowned pirates were washed up on shore the next day. The wreck was discovered in 1984.

TRUE OR FALSE?

Pirates flew a flag called the Jolly Roger. **True or False?**

TRUE! The first pirate flags were plain red, the colour of blood. Some people say that this flag was known in French as *joli rouge* ('pretty red') and that in English this became 'Jolly Roger', a term later used for any pirate flag.

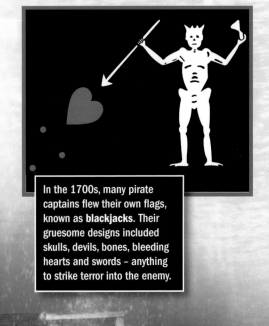

In the 1700s, many pirate captains flew their own flags, known as **blackjacks**. Their gruesome designs included skulls, devils, bones, bleeding hearts and swords – anything to strike terror into the enemy.

CUTLASSES AND CANNON

Whenever they got the chance, pirates would steal swords or pistols. With these they could kill their enemies, terrify their victims – and swagger through the streets and taverns of their favourite places, such as Port Royal, Jamaica.

CUT-THROAT WEAPONS

Pirates fought with all sorts of daggers, axes and swords. The first buccaneers of the Caribbean used long hunting knives. The **cutlass** of the 1700s and 1800s was a short slashing sword, either straight or with a very slight curve. It was used by navy crews as well as by pirates.

The famous pirate Blackbeard fights his last battle in 1718 with pistols and a cutlass (short sword).

SPARKS AND POWDER

Pistols were used at close range. They were fired with a **flintlock**, a gadget which sent a spark into a small pan of gunpowder. The flintlock **musket**, an early form of long barrelled gun, was used at a distance.

One of the most lethal pirate weapons of the 1700s was a home-made **hand-grenade**, a sphere of iron packed with gunpowder. Ships were fitted with large or small cannon (below), which could be used to attack a fort on shore or an anti-pirate patrol. They fired cannonballs, or small iron balls known as **grapeshot**.

Gunpowder was kept in a store called the **magazine**. One careless spark could blast the whole ship sky high. That was the fate of a ship called the *Oxford* in 1669, whose captain was the buccaneer commander Henry Morgan. The explosion killed more than 250 of his own men. Many others deserted Morgan seeing the tragedy as an omen of bad luck.

TRUE OR FALSE?

Pirates even put gunpowder in their rum. **True or False?**

TRUE! Rum was made in the Caribbean in the 1700s and barrels of the strong alcoholic drink were often captured by privateers and pirates. It was possible to test if the rum had been watered down by mixing it with gunpowder. If the gunpowder would not catch fire, it meant the rum had been diluted. Pirates like Blackbeard sometimes drank their rum with added gunpowder to show just how tough they were!

A flintlock pistol.

AMASING FACT
The golden gun

One French corsair of the 1690s called Antonio Füet ran out of grapeshot, so he loaded up his cannon with gold coins called *moidores* and blasted them across the deck of a Portuguese ship. He was known ever afterwards as 'Captain Moidore'.

IN FOR THE KILL!

The cleverest pirates did not rush into action. Their spies gathered information in ports and harbours, looking out for the ships being loaded with the richest cargoes. They found out when ships were sailing and the routes they were taking.

Pirate captains might stalk their prey for weeks, remaining just out of sight below the horizon. Or they might plan an ambush, suddenly sailing out from behind an island or headland.

PLAN OF ATTACK

STEP 1: FOOL THE VICTIM! Crafty pirates pretend to be a harmless merchant crew or fly the flag of a friendly nation. The pirates keep an eye on their victims using a **spyglass** or telescope.

PIRATE JOKE

Q What did the pirate say when he saw the enemy's guns?

A I musket me one of those!

STEP 2: ACT REALLY SCARY!
When really close, they haul up the dreaded pirate flag. The crew show off their vicious cutlasses and daggers.

Pirates approach a galleon quietly as they prepare to attack.

STEP 3: RUN OUT THE CANNON! The pirates fire a warning shot across the **bows** of the enemy – but avoid a direct hit. If the ship sinks, the treasure is lost. If the masts come crashing down, the ship is not worth stealing.

STEP 4: PREPARE TO BOARD! The pirates now throw **grappling irons** (right) at the ship. These catch in the **shrouds** (part of the rigging) and the timbers. The two ships can now be hauled together.

STEP 5: ASSAULT! The pirates swarm on board and fight hand-to-hand, without mercy. They target the ship's captain, locate the treasure and take prisoners.

AMAGING FACT
A vision of hellfire

When the fearsome Captain Edward Teach (the pirate 'Blackbeard') boarded ships in 1717-18, he carried three pairs of pistols. His long beard was matted in dreadlocks. Tucked in his hat he kept the smoking cords of hemp, which were used as matches to fire cannon.

PIRATE PUNISHMENTS

Horrible punishments were not only carried out by pirates. On merchant and military ships, sailors were sometimes bullied and **flogged**. And many pirates were former navy sailors. That was why pirates saved their nastiest punishments for any captured officers who were known to be cruel. Revenge was sweet.

'Sweating' was a torture game where the victim was pricked with forks and swords in front of flaming candles.

FEEL THE PAIN

Pirates would sometimes torture their victims with whips, daggers or fire until they revealed where treasure was hidden. Or very rarely they would tie them to a rope and drag them under the ship's **hull**. This was called keelhauling and victims usually drowned or bled to death.

The buccaneer leader Henry Morgan would place burning matches between fingers and toes, or spread grease on a victim's face and then scorch it with a flame. It was said that Chinese pirates nailed their victims to the deck. In some parts of the world captives might be sold as slaves.

CAST ADRIFT!

One common punishment used by pirates was to put their captives in a little boat and cast them off, often a very long distance from land. Another was to leave them on a remote desert island, with only a few provisions. This was called being **marooned**.

And if any pirate broke the pirate code and betrayed his shipmates, then the rest of his life – if he survived – would be spent in fear of discovery and revenge.

A doomed pirate is left marooned on a desert island.

This picture shows a a victim being made to walk the plank by pirates.

AMAZING FACT

The pirate who was far too nice

Edward England (or Seegar) was an Irish pirate. In 1720 he captured a merchant ship in the Indian Ocean. When he spared the life of its captain, the other pirates were furious. They marooned him on the island of Mauritius!

TRUE OR FALSE?

Pirates often made their victims walk the plank. **True or False?**

FALSE! Ancient Greek pirates threw their captives overboard, but the stories of later pirates making their victims walk the plank – plunging into the waves to drown or be eaten by sharks – are mostly just stories. Very few captives died this way.

THE ROVING LIFE

Pirates did not spend all their long sea voyages fighting battles and searching for treasure. They spent a lot of the time repairing leaky ships, scrubbing decks, **splicing** ropes and mending sails. It was boring work, especially if the ship was **becalmed** with no wind in its sails. Members of the crew would often start quarrelling and fighting.

HARD TIMES

When excitement came it was generally dangerous – climbing the mast in a storm, battling with giant waves or preventing the ship running aground on a reef. An injury might mean having your mangled leg sawn off by the ship's carpenter, with nothing but rum to kill the pain.

PIRATE JOKE

Q Why did pirates never learn the alphabet?

A They were always stuck at 'c'!

Fresh water might run low, just when the only food on offer was a stale biscuit full of wriggling **weevils**! Sickness and fever were common. Many pirates were killed by a disease called **scurvy** because they had a lack of vitamin C, which is found in fruit and vegetables. Below decks where pirates slept was a dark, damp world. Timbers creaked and groaned, while rats scrabbled and scampered.

GOING ASHORE

Pirates came ashore for fresh supplies, catching birds and turtles for food, or carrying out repairs. At these times the ship was most likely to be attacked by **pirate hunters**.

Pirates get drunk and merry in a tavern on the Atlantic Coast.

TRUE OR FALSE?

Pirate captains always had a parrot on their shoulder. **True or False?**

FALSE! The idea that most pirates had a pet parrot comes from the story books. When these were written in the 1880s, it was the fashion for sailors to bring back parrots from the tropics as souvenirs. In the 1600s and 1700s some pirates may have taught a parrot to say 'pieces-of-eight' – but there is no real evidence that they did!

Pirates liked to return to their own bases, where they could gamble, drink and have a wild time. In the 1700s, New Providence, an island in the Bahamas, was the home of Benjamin Hornigold, 'Calico' Jack Rackham, the brutal Charles Vane and the daring women pirates Mary Read and Anne Bonny.

AMAZING FACT
Pirate kingdoms

Some pirates set themselves up as rulers of their own little kingdoms. Abraham Samuel ruled around Fort Dauphin, Madagascar, in the 1690s, while to the north of the island James Plantain built his own fortress and was 'King of Ranters Bay' from 1715-28.

FAMOUS PIRATES

You might think pirates would have wanted to lie low, to avoid the pirate hunters. Not so – most of them loved showing off and wanted to be famous at any cost.

☠ **THE MAGICAL MONK** In the 1200s, a French pirate called Eustace the Black Monk terrorised shipping in the English Channel. He was said to be in league with the Devil who could make his ships invisible.

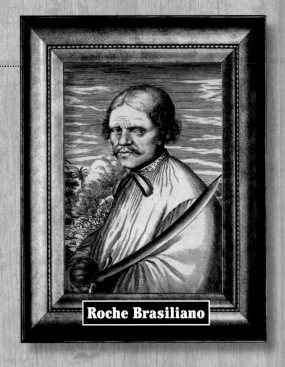

Roche Brasiliano

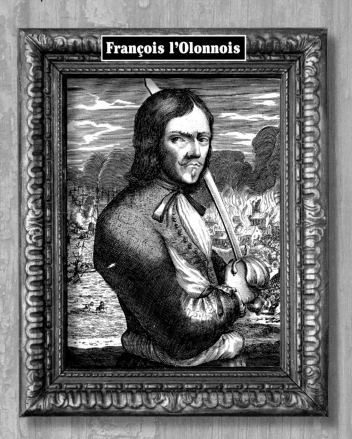

François l'Olonnois

☠ **CRUELLEST IN THE CARIBBEAN** In the 1660s and 1670s, the big Dutch buccaneer Roche Brasiliano was one of the most savage pirates based in Port Royal, Jamaica. He liked to roast his enemies alive. In 1668 the vicious French buccaneer, François l'Olonnois was known for tying rope around people's heads until their eyeballs popped out. He was captured by the native Kuna people on the Spanish Main, torn to pieces and burned.

☠ **THE 'ARCH-PIRATE'** The 'Arch-Pirate' was the name given to Henry Avery, also known as 'Long Ben'. After a brutal attack on the ships of India's Mughal emperor in 1696, his haul of gold, silver and jewels made him the world's richest pirate.

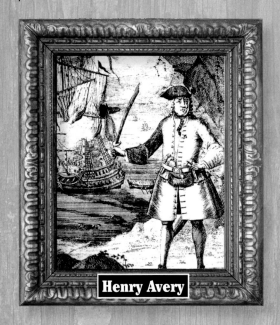

Henry Avery

AMAZING FACT

Fancy threads

It was said that Bartholomew Roberts preferred a nice cup of tea to a bottle of wine – but he was not so sober in his dress. When Roberts was killed off Africa in 1722 he was wearing a fancy waistcoat of crimson silk, gold, diamonds, and a red feather in his hat.

☠ **THE SWASHBUCKLER** Welsh pirate Bartholomew Roberts made his name by sailing into the middle of a **merchant fleet** off Newfoundland, Canada, with all guns blazing, drums beating, trumpets sounding and a blackjack at the mast. His crew was outnumbered 20 to 1! In the chaos that followed, he plundered and burnt many ships and took captives. He is said to have attacked over 400 ships during his short pirate career.

☠ **PIRATE QUEEN** Zheng Yi Sao was a pirate chief on the South China Sea in the 1800s. Her fleet included 1,800 boats crewed by over 80,000 pirates!

Bartholomew Roberts was killed in 1722 when his ship came under attack from the Royal Navy (above). His death was caused by a grapeshot which struck him in the throat.

BURIED TREASURE

When pirates raided ports or shipping, they would steal anything that was immediately useful, such as weapons, medicine chests, tools or supplies. Bulky cargoes such as sugar or tobacco could be sold for good money, but the best plunder was valuable, easy to divide up amongst the crew, easy to hide and easy to sell.

PRECIOUS PLUNDER

Jewels, crosses from churches, or bars of gold and silver from the slave mines of South America were ideal. Money was made of real gold and silver in those days, and coins known as **doubloons** and pieces-of-eight formed part of many a pirate's treasure along the Spanish Main.

SECRET HOARDS

Most pirate treasure was sold off quickly, but for hundreds of years people have been fascinated by tales of treasure chests buried on remote islands and of secret maps showing where they were hidden.

Treasure hidden *from* pirates has been discovered. Some treasure was found in 1927 in a church in Panama. It was probably hidden there in 1671, when the buccaneers of Henry Morgan were rampaging through the city. Treasure from pirate shipwrecks has also been discovered – but endless searches for chests buried on remote desert islands have been unsuccessful.

KIDD'S TREASURE

The famous Captain William Kidd (right) (1645-1701) was a Scottish pirate-hunter and privateer accused of carrying out illegal piracy. Kidd was believed to have left large amounts of buried treasure. He did bury a small hoard on Gardiners Island, New York, but it was recovered shortly afterwards. The remains of his ship, the *Quedagh Merchant*, was found in the Caribbean in 2007. His treasure chests? People have hunted for them in vain, from Canada to Vietnam.

AMAZING FACT
One very big mistake

In 1681 Captain Bartholomew Sharp attacked a Spanish treasure ship called the *Rosario*, off the coast of Peru. He found a fortune in rough silver from the mines – but mistook it for tin! Some of it was made into bullets and the rest was mostly melted down or thrown away.

Captain Kidd instructs his men to bury some treasure.

THE BITTER END

Throughout history, captured pirates have been treated without mercy. Punishments have included crucifixion (being nailed to a wooden cross), drowning by the rising tide, or beheading. In Hamburg in the 1500s, the executioner took just 45 minutes to chop the heads off 33 members of a German pirate band led by Klein Henszlein.

END OF AN AGE

Navy patrols eventually cleared the Caribbean islands of piracy. In 1718 Blackbeard himself was hunted down. He fought bitterly to the end. His head was then cut off and tied to the bows of the victorious captain's ship.

> Blackbeard's severed head was hung from the bowsprit of a Royal Navy sloop so that the captain Lieutenant Robert Maynard could collect his reward.

In the 1700s, hundreds of captured pirates were tried in court and hanged. Their bodies were covered in tar to prevent them rotting and left dangling by harbour walls and river mouths, as a warning to all seafarers who sailed by.

In the 1800s and 1900s, life for pirates became harder and harder. Navy patrols reached even the most remote islands and bays around the world.

THE ONES THAT GOT AWAY

Most pirates met a wretched end. Many died of plague or fever. Many were drowned at sea, or were killed or badly wounded in battle. Some returned home to beg or die in poverty. And just a few, a very few, got away with it, retiring to enjoy their ill-gotten gains... or were they perhaps haunted by the horrors of their past?

Punished pirates were sometimes placed in a cage and left to swing in the air until the flesh rotted off them.

AMAGING FACT
A pirate visits the Queen

The galleys of Gráinne Ni Mháille (Grace O'Malley) raided English shipping off the west coast of Ireland in the 1500s. In 1593 the English took Grace's two sons and half-brother as prisoners. Grace was so angry with her enemies that she sailed to London herself and went straight to complain to Queen Elizabeth I! Her dagger was taken away at the door, but the two women had a head-to-head argument. Grace ended up sailing away safely, with a deal to get her relatives released from captivity!

PIRATE JOKE

JUDGE 'Do you plead guilty to being a pirate?'

ACCUSED 'I'm a bank clerk, m' lord, and if any man says otherwise I'll cut him in tiny pieces and throw him to the sha-aa-aarrrrks!'

PIRATES TODAY

We often think of pirates as they were about 300 years ago. In fact many of the old problems that made piracy happen back then are much the same today – poverty, rebellion, **terrorism** and greed. That is why piracy is on the rise once again. Many poor Somali fishermen in East Africa have turned to piracy because they cannot compete with the large amounts of fishing done by big, foreign-owned companies.

RANSOMS

Modern pirate ships are often small boats or **ribs** with powerful motors. The pirates are armed with AK-47 **automatic weapons** and **rocket-propelled grenades (RPGs)**. They board luxury yachts, kidnapping people and demanding ransoms, or killing the owners and stealing their boats, watches, phones, cameras or money.

AMAZING FACT
Big bucks

In 2011 piracy based in Somalia cost the shipping industry and governments worldwide about 7 billion US dollars. On just one day in 2012, Somali pirates were holding 7 large ships and 177 people hostage.

An RPG fires explosive rockets.

Modern pirates from Somalia in East Africa.

Members of the US Navy approach a suspected pirate ship.

Pirates may board large fishing boats and even huge cargo ships or oil tankers. They hold the crew at gunpoint until large sums of money are paid out by the shipping or oil companies. Top trouble-spots include East Africa, South-east Asia and the north-west Indian Ocean.

MODERN PIRATE HUNTERS

International patrols have now been formed to protect shipping and attack the pirates (above). Modern communications and satellites leave few places for pirates to hide – but rescuing hostages is very difficult, and it is often hard to tell pirates from ordinary fishermen or traders.

Navy patrols are carried out to keep areas of the sea free from pirates.

TRUE OR FALSE?

Pirates today are much more ruthless and dangerous than the swashbucklers of old. **True or False?**

FALSE! People sometimes talk about a 'Golden Age' of piracy in the 1600s and 1700s. They remember the romance and the outlandish rogues, but they forget that piracy has always been a cruel and deadly business.

FANTASY PIRATES!

Even in the 1600s and 1700s people loved to read shocking stories about pirate attacks and trials. Popular songs called **ballads** told tales of heroes and villains.

An illustration of a battle taken from Robert Louis Stevenson's famous book *Treasure Island*.

THE BALLAD OF BLACKBEARD

This ballad describes the death of Edward Teach ('Blackbeard') in 1718:

Will you hear of a bloody Battle,
Lately fought upon the Seas,
It will make your Ears to rattle,
And your Admiration cease;
Have you heard of Teach the Rover,
And his Knavery on the Main;
How of Gold he was a Lover,
How he lov'd all ill got Gain?
.....
Brave Maynard was resolv'd to have him,
Tho' he'd Cannons nine or ten:
Teach a broadside quickly gave him,
Killing sixteen valiant Men.
Maynard boarded him, and to it
They fell with Sword and Pistol too;
They had Courage, and did show it,
Killing the Pirate's Crew.
Teach and Maynard on the Quarter,
Fought it out most manfully,
Maynard's Sword did cut him shorter,
Losing his Head, he there did die.

LONG JOHN SILVER AND CAPTAIN HOOK

In 1881 the Scottish writer Robert Louis Stevenson wrote an exciting children's story called *Treasure Island*. This book was a tale of buried treasure, secret maps and the character Long John Silver. Ever since, children have loved to read about pirates.

From the 1880s, pirates were often treated as comedy characters, too. JM Barrie's fantasy *Peter Pan*, created in the 1900s, introduces Captain Hook, whose hand has been eaten by a crocodile and replaced by a hook.

FROM SPARROW TO SPACE

Many films and animations have been made of pirate tales such as *Hook* (right). The *Pirates of the Caribbean* film series has been popular around the world since 2003. These adventure fantasies are based around the swashbuckling character of Captain Jack Sparrow. Science fiction books, films and television series such as *Dr Who* have even imagined pirates in space.

BUT REMEMBER...

We still enjoy fantasy films and silly jokes about pirates in the old days, but it is also worth remembering the real pirates and their lives and deaths. And that was – and is – a very grim story indeed.

PIRATE JOKES

Q Why did you say 'shiver me timbers?'

A Because I'm a nervous wreck!

'Arrrh, doctor, I've got a nasty cough.'

'Well, captain, let's be having a look at your chest.'

'My chest? How did you know where I buried it?'

Captain Jack Sparrow runs for his life in *Pirates of the Caribbean: Dead Man's Chest*.

KNOW
IT
ALL

QUIZ PAGE

How much have you learned from reading this book? Here is a quiz to test your memory.

1) Is a blackjack
(a) a drink made of rum and gunpowder?
(b) a pirate captain's personal flag?
(c) a type of cannon?

2) Which pirate was captain of the *Whydah*?

3) If a pirate suffered from scurvy, should he have
(a) eaten an orange?
(b) combed his hair?
(c) worn an eye-patch?

4) Which African island had its own pirate 'kingdoms'?

5) Are pieces-of-eight
(a) a sort of parrot food?
(b) rowing boats with eight oarsmen?
(c) Spanish coins?

6) Which pirate captain would have glowed in the dark?

7) What name was given to small balls of metal fired from a cannon?

8) In which sea were the earliest recorded pirate attacks?

9) What was the name given to Chinese sailing ships?
(a) a junk
(b) a punk
(c) a hunk

10) Was the Barbary Coast in
(a) North America?
(b) North Africa?
(c) South Australia?

11) Name two women pirates who fought in the Caribbean.

12) Which pirates took their name from a way of cooking meat?

13) Is a cutlass
(a) a sort of sail?
(b) a telescope?
(c) a short sword?

14) Can you unscramble these pirate names?
(a) CRABBALKED
(b) AJACCOLICK
(c) NBONGLE

15) Which pirate was said to have invisible ships?

GLOSSARY

automatic weapon any gun which continues to fire as long as the trigger is pressed

ballad a popular story made into a poem or song

battens thin strips of wood

becalmed unable to sail because of a lack of wind

blackjack the personal flag of a pirate captain in the 1700s

bows the front end of a ship

brigantine a fast, two-masted sailing ship

cargo the goods being carried by a vehicle

creek a coastal inlet or narrow river

cutlass a short slashing sword, sometimes with a slightly curved blade

dhow a wooden ship of Arab design, with an almost triangular sail

discipline training to follow a strict set of rules

doubloon a gold coin issued by Spain and used across the Spanish Main

flintlock a firing mechanism in which a piece of flint is struck against steel. This causes a spark that sets the gunpowder on fire

flog to beat or whip someone severely

galley a wooden ship which can be powered by oars or by sails

grapeshot small balls of iron, shot from a cannon

grappling iron hooks attached to a rope, thrown into a ship in order to drag it closer, for boarding

hand-grenade a small bomb, thrown by hand

hull the main body of a ship including the bottom and sides

junk a flat-bottomed ship used in China with square sails supported by battens

letter of marque a government licence for privateers, allowing them to attack and loot the ships of an enemy country

lucrative bringing in a lot of money

magazine (1) A store for gunpowder (2) The container on a gun which feeds through bullets for firing

maroon to abandon someone on a distant island or shore, as a punishment

merchant fleet a group of ships carrying goods to be traded

musket a type of long-barrelled gun, an early form of the rifle

mutiny a rebellion by crew members against a ship's officers

pirate hunter anyone who hunts down pirates in order to bring them to justice, either for private reward or as a public service

plunder (1) To steal or loot (2) Stolen goods, loot

ransom money demanded for the release of a hostage or of a hijacked ship

rib a rigid-inflatable boat that is light and fast

rocket-propelled grenade (RPG) a rocket with an explosive head, fired from the shoulder

schooner a fast sailing ship with two or more masts

scurvy a disease that causes the gums to swell and bleed

seadog an old sailor with great experience

shrouds supporting ropes attaching the mast to the sides of a ship

skull and crossbones a particular design of blackjack, showing a skull with two human bones

sloop a fast, single-masted sailing ship

splice interweaving strands of a rope, in order to join two ends

spyglass a telescope

terrorism trying to bring about change by terrifying people with acts of violence

weevil a small beetle that often infests stores of food

WANT TO KNOW MORE?

Here are some places where you can find out a lot more about pirates:

WEBSITES

http://brethrencoast.com/Bio.html
A detailed look at some of the most famous pirates in history.

http://www.thepiratesrealm.com/famous_pirates_pirate_history.html
A useful website covering a wide range of topics, with links to reports on modern piracy.

http://www.rmg.co.uk/explore/sea-and-ships/facts/ships-and-seafarers/pirates
The site of the National Maritime Museum at Greenwich, UK, includes a section on piracy.

http://www.piratesinfo.com/History_of_Piracy.asp
This website provides a wealth of information about piracy, from weapons and flags to pirate ships and punishments.

BOOKS

Eyewitness: Pirate, Richard Platt, (Dorling Kindersley 2007)

Pirates and Smugglers, Moira Butterfield, (Kingfisher 2008)

Pirate Diary, Journal of a Cabin Boy, Richard Platt and Chris Riddell, (Walker Books 2011)

Real Pirates: the Untold Story of the Whydah, from Slave Ship to Pirate Ship, Barry Clifford and Kenneth J Kinkor, (National Geographic 2007)

Website disclaimer:
Note to parents and teachers: Every effort has been made by the Publishers to ensure that these websites are suitable for children, that they are of the highest educational value, and that they contain no inappropriate or offensive material. However, because of the nature of the Internet, it is impossible to guarantee that the contents of these sites will not be altered. We strongly advise that Internet access is supervised by a responsible adult.

INDEX